Offering Meditations

Ray Miles

Biblical quotations, unless otherwise noted, are from the New Revised Standard Version Bible, copyright 1989, Division of Christian Education of the National Council of Churches of Christ in the USA. Used by permission.

Cover and interior design: Elizabeth Wright

10 9 8 7 6 5 4 3 2 1   98 99 00 01 02 03

Library of Congress Cataloging–in–Publication Data

Miles, Ray, 1948-
   Offering meditations / Ray Miles.
   p.   cm.
   ISBN 0-8272-2709-4
   1. Christian giving—Meditations. 2. Offertories. I. Title.
BV772.M49 1998
248'.6—dc21
                              97-43297
                                 CIP

about a crucial aspect of their faith. It inspires people toward the goal of closer relationship with God, achieved through giving.

This book is written in the belief that there is much more that can be accomplished by the offertory meditation or stewardship statement as part of the worship service. It can be a time where faith is directly connected to daily life. The offertory meditation is a time to inspire, to educate, to motivate, to lift people. It can challenge them to grow in their faith and in their discipleship.

These offertory statements are provided to help the church improve an important part of the worship service, and to help members grow in faith. Included are meditations to use on some special days of the church year and secular holidays so that people associate stewardship with those times as well as normal times of life. There are also meditations to help people discover a wider breadth of stewardship than simply the offering on Sunday morning. Though designed to increase the financial offerings in the church, they are intended to be used as a part of a

Introduction

Stewardship meditations have long [been]
treated as an apologetic afterthought in wo[rship.]
Some congregations have even done awa[y with]
meditations as an embarrassing reminder [of the]
material financial situation of the church[. In an]
effort to feel purer and more spiritual, th[ey try]
not to draw attention to it.

Other congregations receive offerin[gs only]
for fiscal survival. The fear is that if the w[eather]
is bad and people are not in church, o[r the]
service is canceled to be part of a de[nomina-]
tional or ecumenical event, the congre[gation's]
finances will suffer irreparable harm. Th[e offer-]
ing is needed but is presented with a r[eluctant]
sense of apology.

This book offers the person in [charge,]
clergy or lay, the opportunity to do m[ore than]
trot out familiar old trite scriptural re[ferences]
and repeat them with no explanation, [applica-]
tion, or inspiration. It gives the churc[h the op-]
portunity to motivate people in their [financial]
giving. It presents the chance to educa[te]

year-round stewardship approach that includes a planned financial stewardship campaign each year.

To complement these meditations, a rich collection of offertory prayers is included in *Chalice Worship*, published by Chalice Press. (See pp. 392–404.) These may be used as written or as patterns for writing your own prayers to go with the meditations.

The traditional understanding in the church is that we are stewards of gifts and resources which belong to God. Jesus refers to each of us being asked at some point to account for the way we used the resources entrusted to us. (Matthew 25)

Stewardship is managing the resources, which belong to God, so that God will be pleased when we account for what we have done. Let us use what God has entrusted to us in appropriate ways.

Sometimes we think that we no longer have to pay any attention to Old Testament laws, especially the one about tithing or giving 10 percent of our income. We claim that we live under the new covenant established by Jesus which frees us from the Old Testament law.

Jesus, however, said, "Do not think that I have come to abolish the law or the prophets; I have come not to abolish but to fulfill....whoever does them and teaches them will be called great in the kingdom of heaven." (Matthew 5:17 and 19b)

It's worth considering as we present our gifts to God this day.

There are two questions to consider as we think about the possessions that we hold in our lives. One of them is, "What are my possessions doing for me?" That's the classic question of the investor and the person trying to build a secure future. "What is the return on investment or the yield produced?"

The other question is one asked by Christians: "What are my possessions doing to me? Are they making me more or less like Jesus my Lord?"

Let us now present our offerings this morning.

4

Giving is a part of worship but the size of the gift is not what makes it worship. A person's worship is not better because he or she gives a bigger gift. God expects you to give, but not more than you can afford.

Think of what God has done for you and what you would like to do for God. God says not to appear at worship empty-handed, but "all shall give as they are able, according to the blessing of the Lord your God that he has given you." (Deuteronomy 16:16b–17)

Now is the time to give according to the blessing you have from God.

The God who made the world and everything in it, he who is Lord of heaven and earth, does not live in shrines made by human hands, nor is he served by human hands, as though he needed anything, since he himself gives to all mortals life and breath and all things." (Acts 17:24–25)

Paul, as he spoke to the Greeks in Athens, speaks directly to us about giving if we are willing to hear it. We don't give because God needs our money. Instead, we give because God first gave to us, gives us life, gives us what we need to live, and gives us all things.

Give offerings in thanks, praise, and worship of the God who doesn't need our money but eagerly desires our hearts.

G iving thanks to God the Father at all times and for everything in the name of our Lord Jesus Christ." (Ephesians 5:20)

Stewardship is a matter of putting the things of life into the proper perspective. In life we tend to get things all fouled up and place too much importance on some issues and not enough on others. Here we are told to give thanks always, in everything. It's a reminder for us to have the most important thing in life, our relationship with Jesus as Lord and Savior, secure. In spite of anything else that occurs, that is the most important. We need to keep it primary in life. We need to express our thanks for that relationship, whether all else is falling around us, or everything is going perfectly.

Let us now in this worship service express our thanks to God with offerings.

Throughout the Old Testament there is the idea that a portion of the world is set aside, separated and dedicated to God. In the Garden of Eden, everything was given to humankind except the tree of the knowledge of good and evil. It was kept separate for God. The Old Testament tithe was one-tenth of a person's produce or income, set aside and kept separate for God. What part of your life and your resources are set aside, separated, and kept exclusively for God?

Now is the time to give God that portion which has been kept separate for God.

8

More than once Jesus reminds us that one of the ways to attain spiritual heights is to be a good steward of our material possessions. If you practice good stewardship of finances, God will give you more and more faith resources to use. Listen to the words of Jesus as you think about your gifts and offerings this morning.

"Whoever is faithful in a very little is faithful also in much;...If then you have not been faithful with the dishonest wealth, who will entrust to you the true riches?" (Luke 16:10–11) If you want the true riches of God, which are valued beyond price, then be faithful with the resources of the world, ones which really matter little to God.

As the people began to provide a place to center their religious faith, Moses related to the people the commandment from God about the tabernacle they were proposing to build.

"Take from among you an offering to the LORD; let whoever is of a generous heart bring the LORD's offering.... And they came, everyone whose heart was stirred, and everyone whose spirit was willing, and brought the LORD's offering to be used for the tent of meeting, and for all its service, and for the sacred vestments." (Exodus 35:5, 21)

Some of this offering will be used to provide for the expenses of the church. That's what God intended to happen with some of the offerings given. Let us give now to support Christ's church and its work.

L yle Schaller in a recent book has a cartoon which describes the tithe as "God asking for just enough to make us pray over how we spend the rest."

Being a steward doesn't mean giving God a little bit of our money. Instead it means we use all our resources in ways that please God and do God's will.

Give generously and pray diligently about how to use the resources God has entrusted to you.

S tewardship is closely connected with giving. It may not always be money that is given. When Peter and John were in the temple after the day of Pentecost, they were approached by a beggar. "But Peter said, 'I have no silver or gold, but what I have I give you...'" (Acts 3:6) Peter then used the gift of healing that God had given him, and the beggar was healed.

As you are asked to give, be creative, ask yourself, "What gifts has God given me that I might give?" Stewardship asks for us to take careful inventory of the assets of our lives, of the gifts, talents, and abilities we have, of the time that we are entrusted with, and then say, "What I have I give to God and to the people of God."

12

E xodus 35:29 tells us, "All the Israelite men and women whose hearts made them willing to bring anything for the work that the LORD had commanded by Moses to be done, brought it as a freewill offering to the LORD."

What does your heart tell you to do? We decide so often how to use our money by reasoning, by financial planning, by resources available, and those kinds of criteria. But what does your heart tell you to do? Do you want to give God more of your life? Do you want to do more to help people who need the gospel? Then do it as a freewill offering to the LORD, as your heart tells you.

Acts 4:32 is a hard verse for us to accept. It says "Now the whole group of those who believed were of one heart and soul, and no one claimed private ownership of any possessions, but everything they owned was held in common." It may not be a command which we are to follow to the letter, but it indicates that following Jesus does mean a radical readjustment of your financial priorities. The ministries of the church, the mission of God and the needs of others become the highest calling upon your resources. For the first Christians it meant all of their resources were used for that.

How has the acceptance of Jesus as Lord and Savior affected the way you prioritize and use your money?

14

At one time in college boat racing, participants were very intent on giving their all to the race. When one of them broke an oar or lost an oarlock, he would jump overboard. The reason was that if he could not stroke to pull his own weight, he would at least relieve the boat of his dead weight.

In the church, the tithe to God is designed so that all will pull their own weight. We don't want anyone quitting the church because they feel they cannot give enough, but we also do not want anyone riding and not working to do all possible for the success of the church.

As we give our offerings this morning, we do so to be a part of the effort we do together for our Lord.

Why don't we use the word *charity* in the church anymore? In later translations of the Bible, charity is replaced many times by the word *love*. Perhaps the translators felt it would help us understand the meaning better.

We've lost something, though, for charity is one way we do love. Perhaps the work of the church would be improved if we started to use the words love and charity together more often. Charity may be an old-fashioned word, but it's a very current way to do love.

The role of sacrifice in offerings is extremely complex, but it is very biblical. David was about to build an altar to worship God. Because he was King, the site was offered to him as a gift. David refused, saying, "I will not take for the LORD what is yours, nor offer burnt offerings that cost me nothing." (1 Chronicles 21:24)

David knew that an offering that had no sacrifice or cost was not worthy of God. As you present your offerings to God, ask if they cost you anything.

We live our lives dreaming of the day when we will do something significant and great for God. The day we win a lottery, the day we earn a million dollars, the day we retire, the day the kids are through college, the day when we have more than we need, *then* we will do something for God. Until then we feel we need every penny we can get hold of in order to make it.

Jesus "looked up and saw rich people putting their gifts into the treasury; he also saw a poor widow put in two small copper coins. He said, 'Truly I tell you, this poor widow has put in more than all of them; for all of them have contributed out of their abundance, but she out of her poverty has put in all she had to live on.'" (Luke 21:1–4)

The widow knew the importance of giving when the opportunity came, rather than waiting to make a big splashy gift. The opportunity to worship God through giving is now. Let us present our gifts and offerings to God.

Numbers 15:3 suggests three different situations when offerings to God are considered appropriate:

"To fulfill a vow," in other words, when we give because we are required by our faith to do so; "as a freewill offering," in other words, when we just want to give to God, regardless of the reason; "at appointed festivals," in other words, when it is part of the order and way we worship God.

As you present your offering this morning, is it done because it is part of your responsibility as a Christian, is it an offering you just want to give to God, or is it because it is a part of the way to worship God? Whichever the situation, it is appropriate and appreciated by your God.

Stewardship doesn't stop when you drop your gift in the collection plate. The mission God has given us is not to give money, but together as the church to feed the hungry, care for the homeless, comfort the grieving, cheer the lonely, preach the gospel, and help people grow as disciples.

To do that, we must be sure, as wise and careful stewards, that our gifts to God are used for the purposes of God. As you give your gift, become involved in the ministries and mission being done with that gift. Give yourself as well as your money.

Remember the ancient mythical figure Midas, who was gifted so that anything he touched turned to gold? I know people who are like that. Everything they do seems to produce financial rewards. They can make money, it seems, from anything.

Do you ever think of that as a gift from God? Did you ever think the ability to make money and gain wealth is a God-given talent? More important than making money is the response to the question "Why make money?" How do you use the ability you have, be it great or small, to make money?

A nd whatever you do, in word or deed, do everything in the name of the Lord Jesus, giving thanks to God the Father through him." (Colossians 3:17)

So many times when we offer thanks to God, we offer thanks for what we have received. Do we ever thank God for what we have the opportunity to do? We have the chance to make a difference in people's lives. We have the opportunity to introduce people to the love of God through Jesus. We have the calling to touch the lives of people with love and fill the needs that they have.

Suppose we give thanks for our opportunities and for the things we do, whatever we do in the name of Jesus. Give thanks for the chance to do it.

In the Garden of Eden, the evil or sin came when the part of the creation kept separate for God was taken by humankind.

"All tithes from the land, whether the seed from the ground or the fruit from the tree, are the LORD's; they are holy to the LORD.... All tithes of herd and flock, every tenth one that passes under the shepherd's staff, shall be holy to the LORD. Let no one inquire whether it is good or bad, or make substitution for it; if one makes substitution for it, then both it and the substitute shall be holy and cannot be redeemed."

Leviticus 27:30–33 talks about the holy aspect of what is set aside as God's portion. It can't be taken or traded. There are to be no substitutions of something inferior for the better which has been set aside for God.

One of the sins we encounter in life is when we try to use for ourselves or our own purposes the portion which belongs to God. Don't hold back, but give freely and joyously the portion of life's goods which truly belong to God.

S tewardship is deciding what is important. Setting the priorities of life is the task of the steward. Listen to what Jesus said to us about priorities.

"Consider the lilies of the field, how they grow; they neither toil nor spin, yet I tell you, even Solomon in all his glory was not clothed like one of these. But if God so clothes the grass of the field, which is alive today and tomorrow is thrown into the oven, will he not much more clothe you— you of little faith? Therefore do not worry, saying, 'What will we eat?' or 'What will we drink?' or 'What will we wear?' For it is the Gentiles who strive for all these things; and indeed your heavenly Father knows that you need all these things. But strive first for the kingdom of God and God's righteousness, and all these things will be given to you as well." (Matthew 6:28b–33)

The most important pursuit is Jesus and then believing God will supply whatever else you need. Let us present our gifts this morning as part of our pursuit of Jesus.

We need to develop new understandings of stewardship for the world in which we live. Some have suggested we think of ourselves as partners with God. As in any partnership, each contributes what he or she has toward the common goal. We give our resources, our talents, our time, and our energies. God contributes other gifts, and together we work toward the accomplishment of the kingdom of God.

God, your partner, asks for your contributions now.

Many of you could repeat John 3:16 from memory. "For God so loved the world that he gave his only Son, so that everyone who believes in him may not perish but may have eternal life." Try reading it a different way, though. Try reading it, "For God so loved the world that he gave..." and then stopping. As we think about our stewardship and our giving to God, we need only think that God loved, so God gave. We love God and other people, so we give. As you present your offerings now, do so because you love God. "For I so love God that I give..."

When, besides this time in our worship service, can we be financial stewards? Many people think the only time they can give to God and support the church they love is in the Sunday offering. More and more people are discovering they can make significant gifts to God's church by estate planning and by naming the church in their wills. Financial stewardship goes far beyond Sunday morning. Let us be the financial stewards for Christ's church.

(To do this, contact your denominational office for advice about who can assist you in this type of planning.)

Stewardship involves recognizing what is important. One story Jesus told illustrates that discovery.

"The kingdom of heaven is like treasure hidden in a field, which someone found and hid; then in his joy he goes and sells all that he has and buys that field." (Matthew 13:44)

Once you recognize how important the kingdom of God is, you'll give everything you have to be sure you keep the kingdom. As you give, be aware of how important God's kingdom is.

It feels good to give! Look at the joy that comes from giving during the Christmas season. Part of the nature God created within us is to be giving and to feel good about that.

1 Chronicles 29:9 tells us "the people rejoiced because these had given willingly, for with single mind they had offered freely to the LORD."

As we ask you to give this morning to God and to the work of Christ's church, we want you to feel good about it. It is good to give.

He looked up and saw rich people putting their gifts into the treasury; he also saw a poor widow put in two small copper coins. He said, 'Truly I tell you, this poor widow has put in more than all of them; for all of them have contributed out of their abundance, but she out of her poverty has put in all she had to live on.'" (Luke 21:1–4)

There are things more important than life. For some, quality of life is more critical than length of life. Survival is not the most important thing. The widow was willing to risk survival because worshiping God through giving was more important to her. For you and me our giving is seldom a question of survival. It is a question of something more important than survival. Let us present our offerings to God.

30

How much of your energy is used for the purposes of God? We devote our energy to our work, to our recreation, to our families, and to other issues. That is right and good and in accordance with God's plan. But how much do we work on faith issues? Of all the energy we use in life, how much do we spend on the ministries and mission of God?

Stewardship involves what we do with everything we have, including our energy.

Take care that you do not forget the LORD your God, by failing to keep his commandments, his ordinances, and his statutes, which I am commanding you today. When you have eaten your fill and have built fine houses and live in them, and when your herds and flocks have multiplied, and your silver and gold is multiplied, then do not exalt yourself,...Do not say to yourself, 'My power and the might of my own hand have gotten me this wealth.' But remember the LORD your God, for it is he who gives you power to get wealth." (Deuteronomy 8:11– 14a, 17–18)

The caution issued to us here is not to think ourselves totally self-sufficient. One reason we receive an offering in worship is to remind ourselves that it is God who has provided the resources. This morning as we receive our offerings, "take care that you do not forget the Lord your God...."

Never for one minute believe that the church asks for your time, your money, your talents simply because it needs these things. The church asks for your time, talents, and possessions because this is the heart of Christian witness.

Please give of your resources to God and the work of God's church.

I will give you the keys of the kingdom of heaven, and whatever you bind on earth will be bound in heaven, and whatever you loose on earth will be loosed in heaven." (Matthew 16:19)

The task we have, as the church after the time of Peter, continues to be awesome and powerful. We have the opportunity to affect eternity for people in our midst and in our world. The interesting question coming from this is, "How do we loose things and how do we bind things today?" When we restrict the ministries of the church by insufficient funding, do we bind the kingdom of heaven? When we are generous and enable the church to do the ministries needed in our world, do we set loose the kingdom of heaven? Our giving has an eternal impact.

No one shall appear before me empty-handed." (Exodus 23:15b)

Many people have decided that worship has nothing to do with giving. They feel that the offering takes away from the mood and atmosphere of worship. That's not what God feels. God knows you cannot worship without giving. It is integral to what worship is, offering ourselves and our resources to God. Consequently, God directed that people not come before him unless they were prepared to give. Now is the time to worship God through our giving.

Richard L. Owenly, in *A Christian and His Money*, published around 1950, said, "It is pure paganism to invest money with no concern for what it may do to or for persons. The Christian steward is one who will insist that his investments will enrich lives and not destroy them."

A Christian steward will not only ask what his or her money is being invested in and what it is being used for, but will take a lower return to ensure the dollars are being used in fulfilling God's ministry and mission.

(If questions are raised about this, direct the inquiries to your denomination's finance and stewardship unit, which will be able to give you information on Christian investing and how the church can help a person do that.)

36 Date Used _____

The scribes and Pharisees were groups of people who were concerned about doing exactly what the religious law of the time said they had to do. In modern terms, they were looking for the least they could do and still be "religious." Jesus in another place challenged them about their giving to God in terms of the tithes being so exact that they tithed the spices in their cupboards (Luke 11:42). Matthew 5:20 says, "For I tell you, unless your righteousness exceeds that of the scribes and Pharisees, you will never enter the kingdom of heaven." Jesus tells us, "Don't be thinking about what is required, or what is the least you can do." If you want to enter the kingdom of heaven, then do more than is required. Love more than is required, forgive more than is required, give more than is required.

It's interesting to observe the society in which we live. It teaches that we should continue to accumulate and pile up possessions. We also live in a society which is basically unhappy. I have yet to see a miserly, self-centered, or stingy person who was truly happy. They might be entertained but were not happy with life. They were worried and stressed about their possessions.

On the other hand, a generous person is one whose life is filled with the joy of giving. He or she is happy and receives a new infusion of joy each time a gift is given. Is it because we were created to be givers, and we will never be what God intended until we learn to give freely and without a sense of obligation? Maybe that's what is meant by "Give until it feels good."

I am giving you these commands so that you may love one another." (John 15:17)

How did Jesus love us? If we are commanded to love as Jesus did, we have to ask how he loved.

Jesus loved by giving totally and holding back nothing, not even his own life. As we think of gifts and offerings to the one who gave all for us, we need to remember "...love one another as I have loved you."

As I grew up we used to go camping with an idea firmly planted in our minds by my dad. "Leave the place a little better than you found it." Later backpackers took up the slogan "pack it in and pack it out," meaning take your garbage out with you. I discovered how important that was the first time I hiked many miles to a mountain hot spring to look into the pool and see soft drink cans on the bottom of the pool. It spoiled the grandeur of the wilderness.

God set us here to be caretakers of the earth. It's a matter of our stewardship how we do that.

One of the most distressing sayings of Jesus for middle-class North Americans is "You cannot serve God and wealth." (Matthew 6:24b) In a society so filled with the pursuit of wealth, these are hard words.

But God has always asked people to make a choice about who they will serve. As our stewardship thought this morning, ask if you are serving and seeking God or wealth.

A prince, according to an old story, sent a token of his love to his betrothed, but when it was received it proved to be an iron egg. With disappointment and anger, the princess threw it down. In time, however, her curiosity caused her to examine it closely. Quite by accident her hand touched a secret spring that caused the outer case to open, revealing an egg of brass. Seeking further, she found another secret spring that revealed an egg of silver, which when opened disclosed an egg of gold. When the secret of this was found, it proved to contain a magnificent diamond of rare beauty.

This is true also of stewardship. To the uninitiated and the beginner, it may at first repel or at least appear uninteresting. It touches many people where it hurts. However, as we work at it, study it, and get into it, we discover a treasure of such value it will never be let go. (From *Stewardship in the Bible,* by Orval D. Peterson, published by Bethany Press, St. Louis, 1952.)

Then God said, 'Let us make humankind in our image, according to our likeness.'" (Genesis 1:26a)

The intention of God was that human beings be like God. That is our goal and is important to remember as we think about giving and the reason why we give. The God in whose image we were created is a giving God. Giving is important to us because it is what we were created to do and to become. As you present your gifts to God and to others through the church, remember that it is a way to become again what God intended you to be.

Daniel Webster is quoted as saying, "The most important thought that ever occupied my mind was that of my individual responsibility to God." That is an important aspect of our lives as Christian stewards. Daniel Webster has helped us see how important it is.

Today ask about your individual responsibility to God and how important it has been to you.

Job in his self-examination to find out why his life had fallen apart looks at all the things that he knows would be contrary to what God wants in a life. As a part of that process he looks at the place of finances in his life.

"If I have made gold my trust, or called fine gold my confidence; if I have rejoiced because my wealth was great, or because my hand had gotten much...this also would be an iniquity to be punished by the judges, for I should have been false to God above." (Job 31:24–25, 28)

Each of us needs to constantly examine the value we place upon wealth as opposed to the place God occupies in our lives. Job knew that wealth could not be the most important thing. Let us give according to what we know to be important, our faith in God.

God is concerned about the stewardship or management of the time you have. The concern comes voiced in the command that we do our work in six days and then spend one day in rest and renewal. The world today seems to be so filled with demands upon our time that it is hard to spend one day simply refreshing ourselves.

As you present your monetary gifts and offerings this morning, think of how you spend time renewing yourself. God wants you to be sure to do that.

One tendency we have is to feel that some-day when we reach spiritual maturity, our giving will reflect that higher plane. The reality is that the ideal never happens.

Jesus knew how to change people. If you want to be spiritual, give your money to God and God's work, then your heart, your interests, and your passions will be there also. Jesus didn't say, "Where your heart is, there your treasure will be." He didn't say, "When your heart is right, your giving will be right also." In fact, he said just the opposite. In order to get your heart right, give your treasure. "Where your treasure is, there your heart will be also." (Matthew 6:21)

Now is the time to move your heart closer to God by means of your offerings.

S ecrecy about giving has been twisted in our
church experience to the point where we take
pride in no one knowing what we do in financial stewardship.

"Whenever you give alms, do not sound a
trumpet before you, as the hypocrites do in the
synagogues and in the streets, so that they may
be praised by others....But when you give alms,
do not let your left hand know what your right
hand is doing, so that your alms may be done in
secret; and your Father who sees in secret will
reward you." (Matthew 6:2–4)

When Jesus talked about giving in secret,
it was to deal with those who gave so they would
be noticed and have a fuss made over them. He
was talking about those who took unhealthy
pride in having others see what they did.

Concern yourself more over the attitude of
your heart and the reason why you are giving,
than in keeping the amount you give secret. Now
humbly, with no pretense or calling of attention,
present your gifts to God.

Being color-blind leaves a person poorer. It's not a condition wherein one doesn't see any color. It's one in which certain colors cannot be distinguished from others. It leaves a person unable to appreciate the radiance of a flower in the foliage of a bush. It leaves someone unable to catch the full wonder in a beautiful sunset and seeing only two or three colors of the full spectrum in a rainbow. How wonderful it would be for that person to see the world in all its color.

There are parallels with a person who sees only a world colored by his or her own self-centered needs, who through a blindness of the soul is unable to see the needs in the world. How wonderful it would be if that person could see the whole world as it really is—filled with needs crying to be met by his or her resources.

Pray that God will heal your soul so you can realistically see what God is calling you to see.

Have you ever considered that there may be gifts offered to God that aren't acceptable to God? We've learned somehow to think of God as eagerly begging for whatever we will give. Remember in Genesis 4:5 that Cain's offering to God wasn't accepted.

King Hezekiah told the people of Israel that after they were consecrated they could offer sacrifices and offerings. (2 Chronicles 29:31) First, consecrate yourself by offering God your heart and life; then your offering to God will be acceptable and pleasing to God.

There are differing ways to see the world and to see the economic construction of the world.

The socialist says the earth and its resources belong to the people as a whole, and not to individuals. They are to be used for the good of people as a whole.

The communist says everything belongs to the state, and it is the state that must benefit from their use.

The capitalist says the economy is based upon private ownership of wealth and the potential to accumulate is unlimited. The wealth is used to generate more wealth.

The Bible says, "The earth is the LORD'S and all that is in it, the world, and those who live in it." (Psalm 24:1)

As Christians we present our offerings to the Lord because God has a claim before all else.

Have you ever considered the idea that as you gain increased resources, God calls you to give an increased proportion of those resources? Not an increasing amount, but an increasing proportion. Jesus said, "From everyone to whom much has been given, much will be required; and from the one to whom much has been entrusted, even more will be demanded." (Luke 12:48b)

Could that mean that as you get more resources God expects an even bigger proportion? What is the proportion of your resources that you give? Has that proportion changed lately?

Have you tuned your car lately so that the emissions are below government standards? What do you do with leftover pesticides, housecleaning products and the like? The regulations for safe disposal are complicated and sometimes seem to be a real hassle, but these questions are faith questions and stewardship questions.

If you believe that God created the earth and put human beings in charge of caring for it, then the pollution of the environment and the wasting of the resources of the earth are issues of our relationship to God.

Stewardship is more than money. It's responsible care for the Earth and the things on it that God has delegated to us.

Often people ask whether they should calculate their giving to God to include charities other than the church. That's an individual decision, but the Bible has some guidance. Throughout the Old Testament, the rules about giving have a clear distinction between what is given to God and what is for charity. Tithes were what God asked, offerings were what people decided to do in addition.

When in the worship service we ask for tithes and offerings, we are asking for two different things. We are asking for what you have committed to give God and also for what you have decided out of love to do in addition.

Shall we present our tithes and offerings to the Lord?

An elder in a certain church was a great servant of Christ. He was superintendent of a large Sunday school, preached a great deal, and was a baker by trade. Once when he was traveling on a train, a zealous woman passenger asked him bluntly, "Are you a Christian, sir?" He replied that he was. After she had thanked God for this, she asked him, "What work are you doing for the Master?" "I bake," he replied. "I did not ask about your trade, but what service you give to him who redeemed you?" the woman said. "I bake, madam," he answered.

This Christian baker's reply was sincere and went to the root of a true conception of stewardship. The common things of life, when dedicated to Christ, become holy, and daily service becomes a vehicle for the greatest expression of a life's devotion. This baker made his baking contribute to the spiritual purposes of God.

This morning the challenge is to make your life and the things you do contribute to the spiritual purposes of God.

J esus is sending his followers out on their mission as told in Matthew 10:7−8. "As you go, proclaim the good news, 'The kingdom of heaven has come near.' Cure the sick, raise the dead, cleanse the lepers, cast out demons."

The ministries we are to perform as followers of Jesus are clear: evangelism, healing, bringing new life, helping people overcome the horrors of their lives. Those ministries in today's world take money. Jesus was not unaware of that need and in the next verse urged the disciples to do the ministry without worrying about money. The ministry to which many of us are called is to provide the financial resources so others can do those specific ministries without worrying about money. Whether overseas or in this community, there are people doing ministry on our behalf. They need to be freed of the worry over finances. What is the calling of God to you?

A phrase often used in connection with the elements of communion is "The gifts of God for the people of God."

The offering we take now is the opportunity for the people of God to give the gifts to God.

Shall we present our offerings now to God, who has already given us unmeasurable gifts?

In the early church, the bread and the wine used for the celebration of the eucharist were brought to the table along with the other offerings of the people. Through the blessing and mystery of God, the ordinary elements of bread and wine took on holy significance and great power.

God still takes the ordinary offerings of people and blesses them. They then become powerful as the tools and the means to do the ministries of Christ. Shall we present our offerings to God for blessing and empowering to be used in the mission of Christ?

Stewardship Meditations
for Special Days
and Seasons

Advent

A dvent is the period of preparation for the coming of Christ. It is the time to get ready for Christmas. The celebration of Christ's birth takes a time of planning ahead of the celebration. That time is Advent.

As we go through Advent we need to make plans for what we will give. Preparation takes time, and as we head toward the celebration of the birth of Jesus and toward a New Year, prepare yourself for celebrating and for giving.

Christmas

Christmas is a time when giving is a major matter. What shall we give? To whom do we give presents? Have we got all the presents ready for giving? Will our gifts bring pleasure to the recipients? Have we gotten gifts for everyone who gave one to us?

Through all the giving of this season, the reminder to us is that God's gift was salvation through the person of Jesus.

As we approach Christmas this year, have we considered what gift we will give to God?

Christmas or Epiphany

The story of the Magi has been romanticized and elaborated in many ways. There's the addition of the legend of the fourth wise man. The idea of their being kings has been greatly elaborated. Debates and misunderstandings continue about the time of their visit, the length of their journey, etc.

There is no confusion about what they were doing. They came to worship the child and give gifts to Jesus. Piercing all the speculation and discussion of the story about the Magi is the realization that the child they brought gifts to was the Messiah of God come to save humanity. Today we come giving our gifts to God for the wonderful gift God has given us.

New Year's Day

Resolutions are common as we move into the New Year. Many of us make decisions about our lives and the changes we want to make. Some of the changes are in relation to the priorities we have in our lives. We decide to make our lives reflect what is most important.

Some of the resolutions reflect habits and actions we want to change. We vow to stop or start doing something.

Do any of your resolutions touch what you give to God? Is God going to be a higher priority this year? Is your giving going to change this year?

As you make resolutions, consider how they relate to God and your life for God.

First Sunday in Lent

The Lenten season is a time for self examination and discovery of ourselves. It is a time to recognize the sin in our lives and work to change our ways of living. One of the areas so many of us find sinful is the attitudes we have toward money. Greed runs amuck in our lives. As we begin our season of advent this year, might we be looking at our generosity and the greed which we fight in our lives? By being generous we will discover the joy of life which is lived for God and for others and escape the pain of a greedy life. Let us be aware of that now as we present our offerings to God.

Easter

How does a person celebrate new life? How do we celebrate the resurrection of Jesus? That may be one of the hardest questions of Easter.

Many people who have faced death and been given a reprieve treat life with a sense of importance, making life a sacred and holy trust. They approach life with different priorities, with a different sense of what is important, and a new vision of what they want to accomplish. They see a particular reason for life.

In other words, they become better stewards of life. The best way to celebrate Easter is to improve our stewardship of the life we have and the new life we have been given.

Income Tax Time

This is the Sunday closest to April 15 and the deadline for filing tax returns and paying our taxes. It's not a favored activity and is one of the chief sources of complaint for people anytime, but especially now. Jesus was asked about taxes as a trap but also maybe as a hopeful way to get out of paying taxes. "He said to them, 'Then give to the emperor the things that are the emperor's, and to God the things that are God's.'" (Luke 20:25)

We have all diligently taken time to figure and then pay what is due to the government. Have we taken time to figure and pay what is due to God?

Memorial Day

Memorial Day is a day to remember people. It's a time to remember family members who are no longer living. It's a time to remember people who gave their lives for freedom.

It's a good time to remember the church we have inherited. Paul uses the image of being "surrounded by a cloud of witnesses" (Hebrews 12:1) to refer to those who preserved the church so we could have it.

This weekend as we remember, let us ask ourselves also about the stewardship of the church. How do we prepare and preserve the church for those in the future?

Pentecost Sunday

The scripture tells us of the incredible day when God chose to pour out the Holy Spirit upon the followers of Jesus. There was tremendous power and mystery associated with the day and the way God acted upon people. It was a marvelous unveiling of what God can do with people.

We as the church retain that story and tell it time and again. What of the power and the mystery of that day? How have we been stewards of the mysteries of God? Are there ways for us to better manage the gospel and the mysterious grace of God? Managing may not be a word we are comfortable using about the gospel, but the thought is important. How do we care for and use the power God has enabled us to have?

Labor Day

What do you work for? Why do you labor? What are you trying to accomplish? For life to be all that God created it to be, we need to have a goal, a vision, something we are working to accomplish. If you work only to survive, only to provide existence for another day, then your life is hollow and missing something.

God has set us here to make the realm of God a reality. We are here to relieve suffering, work for justice, proclaim the love of the gospel.

Whatever our job, we labor for God. Let us present to God now the fruits of our labor.

World Communion Sunday

In hundreds and thousands of churches around the world today, communion will be celebrated. Around the world, churches will be united in the power of this celebration. The strength of this day comes in part from the unity of the celebration. The strength of the church comes from the people of God uniting to do the mission of God. That strength is magnified when all those Christians combine and pool all their gifts and resources to accomplish the ministry of Christ.

Stewardship is recognizing the power of God through our unity and cooperation as followers of Jesus.

Thanksgiving

The word "thanksgiving" is made of two separate words, "thanks" and "giving." It seems to indicate that there can be no expression of thanks unless there is giving associated with it. As we celebrate our gratitude for all we have and all we have been given, we struggle to find appropriate ways, including feasts, naming our blessings, and offering prayers. Can we find a better way to express thanks to God than through giving?

Index

Genesis

1:26a	42
4:5	49

Exodus

23:15b	34
35:5, 21	9
35:29	12

Leviticus

15:3	18
27:30–33	22

Deuteronomy

8:11–14a, 17–18	31
16:16b–17	4

1 Chronicles

21:24	16
29:9	28

2 Chronicles

29:31	49

Job

31:24–25, 28	44

Psalm

24:1	50

Matthew

5:17, 19b	2
5:20	36
6:2–4	47
6:21	46
6:24b	40
6:28b–33	23
10:7–8	55
13:44	27
16:19	33
25	1

Luke

11:42	36
12:48b	51
16:10–11	8
20:25	64
21:1–4	17, 29

John

3:16	25
15:17	38

Acts

3:6	11
4:32	13
17:24–25	5

Ephesians

5:20	6

Colossians

3:17	21

Hebrews

12:1	65